Capsule Craze

Capsule Wardrobe, Curated Closet, Dream Closet, Confident Closet (Easy Steps, Shopping Right, Makeovers, Style)

Stacy S. Sullivan

Capsule Craze: Capsule Wardrobe, Curated Closet, Dream Closet, Confident Closet (Easy Steps, Shopping Right, Makeovers, Style)

Table of Contents

Book 1 - Capsule Wardrobe

Essential Plan For Creating Your Minimalist Wardrobe

(Dream Wardrobe, Mindful Living, Simple Elegance)

1 - Introduction

In this fast-paced world where no time should be wasted, you can't really spend too much time figuring out what to wear. Due to the fast-changing trends in the clothing industry, it's understandable why a woman would have an overstuffed closet filled with pieces that are trendy today, but not tomorrow. The result, however, is that she stresses over what to wear every day since all she has are statement pieces that aren't interchangeable and are only good for one-time use.

This is one reason why British style icon Susie Faux came up with the capsule wardrobe—to give women style and confidence without necessarily taking up too much of their time getting dressed up. Capsule wardrobe remains popular decades after it was first conceptualized not because it limits the number of clothes a woman has to wear, but also because the limitation in choices allows her to get dressed faster without compromising her personal style.

If the idea of putting together your own dream capsule wardrobe appeals to you, then you've come to the right place. This book contains all the essential information you'll need to start putting up your own capsule wardrobe.

1 - INTRODUCTION

For the next chapter, you'll learn about what a capsule wardrobe is, its benefits, and how Susie Faux came up with the idea.

Another discusses how factors such as your body type, personal style, lifestyle, favorite color palette, and many more can help you decide which clothes to put into your capsule wardrobe.

Next, you'll learn how having a capsule wardrobe can help inspire mindful living. Most people who have built their own capsule wardrobes share that they now have a more heightened sense of consciousness on what they put into their closets. This consciousness helps promote mindfulness, which is particularly helpful when it comes to keeping a capsule wardrobe.

The last chapter shares concrete suggestions on which pieces to put into your capsule wardrobe to keep it simple yet functional.

2 - What Is a Capsule Wardrobe?

A lot of people nowadays continue looking for ways to make use of their time efficiently, and creating a capsule wardrobe is one way. A capsule wardrobe is composed of a finite number of clothes that are often minimalist and are interchangeable. Though the principle behind it is "less is more," the size of a capsule wardrobe depends entirely on what you want. Basically, a capsule wardrobe should consist of high quality clothes that aren't only minimal, but are also clothes that you would love to wear frequently.

A Quick History

Some of us might be hearing the term capsule wardrobe for the first time, but history states that this has been going on since the 70s. While today's capsule wardrobes may have thousands of different varieties to suit different lifestyles, the foundational principle of having interchangeable, minimalist clothes remains basically the same.

The term capsule wardrobe was first coined by British boutique owner Susie Faux, who currently owns a boutique in London called Wardrobe. Growing up surrounded by people who tailor clothes for women, Faux developed a consciousness seeing how well-fitting clothes make a person appear confident and more beautiful.

As a grown up, she started working in the advertising industry, further igniting her passion towards helping other women dress just as well as the males. This led her to open Wardrobe in 1973, waving her battle cry of inspiring women to have confidence and style.

It wasn't until 1980 that the term capsule wardrobe made a debut in Faux's book entitled "Wardrobe: Develop Style and Confidence." Together with a UK-based designer, Jil Sander, she carefully crafted the wardrobe to have a minimalist, foundational aesthetic wherein fewer clothes of higher quality will be included. According to her, a capsule wardrobe creates confidence and success because of the overall look created from high quality pieces.

The book, which was then meant for career women, became like a road map—guiding women to dressing with ease without losing the professional look. For this to be possible, you'll need to have a few core pieces: blouse, coat, bag, belt, dress, jacket, sweater, skirt, trousers, tights, and shoes. While a capsule wardrobe is minimal, there's not standard size of a wardrobe and varies entirely from person to person.

Benefits

The versatility of a capsule wardrobe is not only what makes it popular, but also a few other benefits as well. There are three main benefits of creating your own capsule wardrobe.

First, a capsule wardrobe saves time. Due to the minimal pieces in a capsule wardrobe, getting ready in the morning can be done much faster. Packing for trips can be done in just a few minutes because the pieces you'll bring with you are interchangeable, thus eliminating the need to bring a lot. Also, having few clothes means doing less laundry, so you'll have time to do more important things.

The second benefit of a capsule wardrobe is that it saves energy. A minimal wardrobe reduces the feeling of anxiety and stress from having to choose what to wear every time. In addition, wondering which clothes to pick on a daily basis somehow promotes emotional fatigue. Having only a few choices reduces that fatigue and allows you to spend your energy to focus more on other things.

Lastly, the best benefit you can get from a capsule wardrobe is that it saves you money. Because the pieces in a capsule wardrobe are versatile and can be mixed and matched easily, you won't have to spend as frequently for new clothes. Capsule wardrobes also kick out clothes that can only be worn once, so that's more value for your money there.

In 1985, American designer Donna Karan brought the concept to the United States. She put up her own clothing line—Seven Easy Pieces—which also caters to contemporary career women. The foundational piece of clothing in her line is a black body suit which can be built to a full outfit by adding more pieces.

If you've reached this point and realized that building a capsule wardrobe would be perfect for you, simply head on to the following chapters.

3 - Building Your Dream Capsule Wardrobe

While Faux identifies in her book "Wardrobe: Develop Style and Confidence" some core pieces for a capsule wardrobe, there are no strict rules as to what style and how many pieces you'd like to have. You don't even have to go on a shopping spree to build one. If you're clear on what your fundamentals are and you know exactly what you want, shopping will be made easier and you'll achieve that wardrobe that truly expresses your style, flatters your body, and makes dressing up so much easier for you.

Before you start culling your wardrobe and hitting the stores, here are some tips you'd like to keep in mind when building your dream capsule wardrobe.

Identify Your Body Type

Using a measuring tape, measure your bust, shoulders, hips, and waist. The following are the different body types according to the width of these extremities.

- Heart-shaped – the bust and shoulders are wider than your hips.

- Pear-shaped – the hips are wider than your bust and shoulders.

- Hourglass-shaped – if there's only little difference between the widths of your shoulders and hips.

- Rectangle-shaped – your bust, hips, and shoulders are of the same width (or have very little difference in measurement).

These are the four most common types of body shape. Using these as your reference will help you choose pieces that are flattering and will complement your body.

Find Your Colors

In fashion, it's important to find clothing that'll flatter your skin tone. There are mainly four different skin tones—light cool, dark cool, light warm, and dark warm.

Each of these skin tones has a set of color palettes that are flattering and would greatly serve as a complement. For example, a dark cool skin tone works best with jewel tones (bright colors) while people with light warm skin tones would find pastel colors especially flattering. Try on different colors to see which colors are best for the color of your skin for that confident and polished look.

Defining Your Personal Style

The most crucial part towards building your own capsule wardrobe is knowing what your personal style is. Adopting capsule wardrobe recommendations on Pinterest wouldn't always work if the pieces don't fit your natural, personal style. Narrow down your choices and check which clothes best express who you are. This way, shopping will be less of a hassle and you'll have the confidence to actually wear what you put into your capsule wardrobe.

Consider Your Lifestyle

Capsule wardrobes should suit your lifestyle. Faux mentioned that her book is for career women, which explains why she included trousers, dresses, blouses, and other corporate-looking items as her core pieces.

Consider where you spend most of your time in. Are you an office worker? An on-the-go photographer? Or a gym instructor? Making a list of your daily activities could help you see what your daily life is like, and from there you can narrow down the type of clothes that would suit those activities.

Declutter Your Closet

Scrap out any clothes that you don't use anymore, or those that don't make you feel confident anymore. Note that this'll be extremely challenging, but brutal honesty is a must if you want to rid your closet of all those unwanted clothes to make room for what is truly essential.

After you're done detoxifying your closet, you have the option to donate, store, or throw out your unwanted clothes. Think of this activity as your stepping stone to a fresh, new start, and that you're doing this to make way for pieces that'll only serve to boost your confidence and style.

Create Formulas of Your Dream Outfits

Start thinking about outfit combinations (you can look at Pinterest or Lookbook for inspiration). Building outfit formulas helps make shopping easier, as you already know what pieces you are looking for. Are you a jeans-T-shirt kind of person? Or do you need to have more smart casual pieces? Start your formulas by determining the basic pieces, and pairing them with other items until you achieve your ideal formula.

Go for the Basics

The best, solid foundations for any capsule wardrobe are staple, basic items. You will want to build upon these basic pieces to make great outfits. Think of the basic pieces as the bottom-most part of a pyramid, and the ones on top are the statement pieces. Basic pieces can range anywhere from a white button-up blouse, a pair of black skinny jeans, a beige sleeveless top, and many more.

Include the Shoes

It is important that every capsule wardrobe has a versatile pair of shoes. Ideally, there should be three pairs of shoes that can go with any outfit you can think of in your capsule wardrobe. Do you love masculine shoes such as boots and oxfords? Are you more of a doll shoes type of person or do you prefer heels more? Make sure that the shoes you wear are also comfortable and that the colors go well with your outfits. The safest choices rest with neutral tones such as black, brown, or nude.

4 - Practicing Mindful Living through a Capsule Wardrobe

The journey towards creating your dream capsule wardrobe starts with mindfulness.

Mindfulness is a state where your consciousness is at its peak. You may be wondering what the connection is to creating a wardrobe, but apparently adding and taking out clothes from your closet involves some sort of awareness.

Most people who have created their own capsule wardrobes swear that it helps them become mindful of the clothes they wear, that the clothes aren't just mindlessly bought for the purpose of having something new to wear. Creating a capsule wardrobe doesn't only help you become mindful of the clothes you buy, but also of their quality and purpose.

Here are some tips that can help shift your perspective about the clothes you put in your closet.

Practicing 'Quality over Quantity'

Another principle behind capsule wardrobes is 'less is more.' While you might be thinking why on earth would you have less clothes when the fashion industry is a fast-paced world, a small, minimal closet is actually more functional.

Invest in quality fabrics. The first thing to consider is how the fabric feels in your hand. If the fabric feels nice and drapes well, then it could be a sign that the fabric is of good quality.

Opt for well-made basics. As mentioned previously, basic pieces serve as a solid foundation for all the outfits you will be creating from your capsule wardrobe. Make sure to choose quality, well-fitting basics.

Consider the number of times you can wear a piece. The best technique to creating a functional capsule wardrobe is including pieces you wear in different ways. The more versatile an item is, the more valuable it is to your capsule wardrobe.

Choose the best fit. Don't always pay attention to the size labels since there is no universal sizing chart in the clothing industry. Always buy items that fit you well regardless of the size labels.

Own Your Personal Style

Another mindfulness practice is knowing your personal style, and owning it. This will help you shop for pieces more easily, and will reduce the time and money wasted on clothes that you'll never wear.

Today over tomorrow. Stuffing your closet with clothes, thinking you'd use them in the future is not a mindful practice. Only buy what you are going to be wearing for the present.

Neutrals over loud colors

While it's not a crime to choose clothes with loud colors, keep these choices limited to only a few statement pieces. Choose neutrals as your basics because they're easier to mix and match.

Stick to your style

While there's no harm experimenting, wearing clothes that define your style helps bring out more confidence.

Choose classic, timeless pieces rather than bold, trendy ones

The fashion industry creates trends to inspire more purchases from people. If you stick to basic pieces that will last you years regardless of the trends, you'll be able to maintain a sustainable closet, without the need to buy every time a new trend comes in.

Your Closet Is a Reflection of Your Lifestyle

If you want to keep a mindful closet, it's important that it stays organized. Being conscious of your possessions is nearly impossible if you can't see them all. The first step to an organized closet is decluttering it and taking note of the following.

Display your clothes properly. Nothing defines 'organized closet' as displaying your clothes the way you should. Fold your shirts properly or hang up your coats with care.

Apply the 'one in, one out' principle. If you want to avoid a stuffed closet, take an item out every time you buy new ones. You can either donate it or put it up for sale.

Launder with care. Read the labels on your clothes before throwing them all together in the washing machine. Some fabrics are not meant to go in the washing machine, and doing so will only ruin them. Treat and launder your clothes with care for them to last a lifetime.

Knowing where your clothes are made. While this isn't always followed by all people, some are mindful enough to check out where their clothes are made, particularly whether the workers are treated well by these clothing companies.

While these tips may seem difficult at first, it's pretty easy to maintain a mindful closet once you've started step one. It's advisable to start during the weekend, where you have more free time to become more conscious about your closet. If you can't manage it in one weekend, try adding a bit more consciousness in the next weekends to come and you'll have a more mindful wardrobe in no time.

5 - Basic Pieces to Include in a Simple yet Elegant Capsule Wardrobe

A capsule wardrobe should consist of clothes that will never go out of style. As much as you loved statement pieces before, you should keep these to a minimum if you want to start building your capsule wardrobe. With less options, mostly consisting of basic pieces, you'll be able to plan your outfits more easily. Remember that owning a capsule wardrobe means you'll have clothes that you can wear frequently and interchangeably with the other pieces.

Even though Faux has already shared her core pieces in her book, you are free to tweak it according to your own taste or style. In this chapter, you'll read about a sample capsule wardrobe, and more detailed information on why the basic pieces are essential.

What Should Go Into Your Wardrobe?

The previous sections in this book consisted of basic tips that allow you to adopt the mindset to help you build your own dream capsule wardrobe. This time, you'll read about the staple pieces that serve as the very foundation for build-

5 - BASIC PIECES TO INCLUDE IN A SIMPLE YET ELEGANT CAPSULE WARDROBE

ing a capsule wardrobe.

Here are the suggested capsule pieces:

- 3 bags

- 2 blouses

- 3 coats

- 2 dresses

- 2 pairs of skinny jeans

- 5 pairs of shoes

- 2 scarves

- 2 skirts

- 2 sweaters

- 2 shirts

- 2 tank tops

- 2 work trousers

Bags (3)

A large, spacious bag is necessary for when you need to carry a lot of stuff with you. This is great for when you plan to go on a trip, to the gym, or when you just need to bring a lot of your stuff with you.

Another bag is one that you can bring with you daily, particularly for work. Choose a simple one in a neutral tone so that it can accompany any type of outfit. Choose one that has both a strap and a handle, so you can carry it any way you want.

Lastly, a clutch bag is great for when you need to go on a night out or to formal events.

Blouses (2)

Include a simple blouse and a statement blouse in your closet. The simple one should be in a neutral shade (white, beige, black, or nude) so that it can be used interchangeably with your jeans, trousers, etc. The statement blouse should create a statement look but can still be worn with flat shoes or jeans during the daytime or with trousers and heels at night.

Coats (3)

The reason why you need three coats is because there are different seasons. For the winter, a heavy coat is the best choice, but note that you should keep this in a muted color.

Another type of coat you can include is a camel trench coat that can be worn over any outfit without warming you too much. If you want to go for that effortless chic look, then this is a great addition.

Lastly, a denim jacket is great to wear during the spring and summer season. It's casual enough to wear with jeans and T-shirt, but can also be thrown over a classic dress at night.

Dresses (2)

It's important to buy a dress that can be worn multiple times for different occasions. A classic dress can be paired with sandals or flats during the day, and can still be paired with heels and a clutch bag in the evening. This can also be worn with tights to make it look professional and sophisticated enough for work.

The second type of dress you should have is a patterned

one. This is useful for events such as nights out, dates, or parties. Make sure to choose a patterned dress that can easily be dressed down or dressed up with the right accessories and footwear.

Skinny Jeans (2)

With skinny jeans, you could never go wrong with the colors indigo and black. These are the only classic colors you'll need when it comes to jeans. They can go with any top, and can be leveled up by simply pairing them with the right shoes and accessories.

Shoes (5)

Shoes are often left-out when it comes to keeping a minimal wardrobe, but you don't need to have that many shoes in your closet. All you need are 5 pairs of shoes which can be worn to just about any occasion.

First, you'll need comfy flats. You can slip your flats on easily for the effortless look. Plus, it can be worn with jeans or with a classic dress.

Next, you'll also need pointed flat shoes. Fashion experts

say that wearing pointed shoes adds a touch of elegance to your outfit without compromising the simplicity of a daily look. Wear it with jeans or trousers during the day, or pair it with a dress for an elegant night out look.

Third, a timeless choice would be black boots. Wear them with jeans for that rock chic look, or with a dress for that Gossip Girl flair.

Next, invest in pointed toe heeled pumps that will be your go-to shoes for a sophisticated look. For a dressed up look, pair them with jeans. Wear them with jeans for a casual yet elegant look.

Lastly, a flat sandal (preferably embellished) is a great must-have for summer. It should be neutral in color so it complements any outfit you wear. The embellishments make it wearable even on a summer night.

Scarves (2)

For the winter, a heavy scarf is a must. A knitted one is the best choice as it's great for keeping you warm. Stick to neutral tones once again to make it suitable to wear with any of your outfits.

Also throw in a light scarf that can be used in spring to block out a bit of sunlight. This should be made from light materials such as satin or silk. It can also double as an accessory; simply tie it around your neck as worn by chic French women.

Skirts (2)

For skirts, you should have one that you can wear during the day and one that can be worn at night. The daytime skirt should be flowing and can be worn with a simple blouse or sweater. For an androgynous, casual look, try wearing it with denim jackets and boots.

Sweaters (3)

First, you'll need a simple, lightweight sweater to wear daily. Note that the style should be simple and that the material isn't too heavy so that you can wear it for all seasons.

Next, a patterned sweater is great for when you want to look bolder and more put together.

Lastly, a knitted lightweight sweater is ideal for layering over s and blouses. You can even bring this with you just in case you find yourself a bit chilly during fall.

Shirts (2)

Probably the most staple piece that'll last you a lifetime are shirts. You can make do with only two of these, one white and one black. These two colors are great with almost anything paired with them, and you can dress them up easily with accessories.

Tank Tops (2)

For the summer, you'll need a casual tank top that you can use when the weather's warm. Again, choose a muted color that's comfortable, simple, and can easily be paired with a skirt or a pair of jeans.

The second tank top you should have should be versatile enough to be worn during the evening. For this, choose a dressy tank top, one which you can also wear as a statement piece during the day but can double as a classy, elegant top at night.

Work Trousers (2)

For work trousers, all you need are two colors: black and grey. Grey is the choice color to wear during the months of summer and spring, while black trousers are especially popular during the winter. The great thing about trousers is that they can also make a great evening look when paired with the right heels.

6 - Conclusion

Your wardrobe reflects your personal style, your lifestyle, and how you are as a person. A cluttered, overstuffed closet is most likely a reflection of how disorganized and indecisive you are, especially when it comes to getting ready for the day.

A capsule wardrobe not only limits the number of clothes you own but also helps you become more mindful of what you put into your closet and how you arrange them. As a result, you'll be able to plan your outfits more efficiently, and getting ready in the morning will be faster because you already have your outfit formulas planned beforehand.

Putting together your dream capsule wardrobe may sound intimidating at first. Not only do you have to take out the clothes that don't serve you well anymore, you'll also need to become more discerning of what you buy for your closet in the future. Just take into consideration the tips you've learned in this book and you can easily put together your own dream capsule wardrobe in to time.

Book 2 - Curated Closet

Find Your Personal Style And Create An Amazing Capsule Wardrobe (Minimizing Your Closet, Step-By-Step)

1 - Introduction

One of the most basic needs in life is clothing. But beyond the rudimentary need for protection against external elements, clothes can play a much bigger role. The way you dress is very often an indication of who you are.

The thought immediately goes to uniforms, be it for students or professionals like cops, military or medics. A person in a three-piece suit is going to be perceived in a very different way than someone wearing hoodie and sweatpants. Saying "blue-collar" or "white-collar" is in itself short-hand for different types of labor.

Clothing also has a lot to do with personal expression. Individual fashion choices can signal certain things. Someone who is very feminine can opt for clothes that are pink or with floral patterns. Someone with elegant and refined taste may feel their best and most confident in a suit and tie, while someone else thinks that the best things to wear are a plain T-shirt and denim jeans. As fashion designer and stylist Rachel Zoe puts it, "style is a way to say who you are without having to speak."

This book will teach you how to have a curated closet through defining and refining your personal style. To push that concept further, you can even opt to have a very pared down, minimal look with the help of a capsule wardrobe.

Having a limited choice when it comes to fashion may seem counterintuitive, especially with the way that fashion is often marketed as having everchanging styles and trends. But the beauty of being able to define your personal style is that your look will be distinctive in itself, even if you choose not to hop on to the latest trend. It's also a real powerful move to have a signature look.

With simple steps, you can start the journey towards a curated closet full of clothes that fit your aesthetic and lifestyle. These are the clothes that will make you feel comfortable, beautiful and that you'll want to keep and wear forever.

2 - Reflection

A lot of decluttering challenges on the internet begin with taking all items and dumping them into one place. We'll get to that, too. But before this, you should reflect first and be truly honest about two essential things. First, what do I want to achieve with my capsule wardrobe? Second, what kind of person am I?

The first question targets aspirations and will define what items should be prioritized. The second one gets to the basics and eliminates choices right away very quickly. Let's answer that one first.

Knowing Yourself

Your answer to the question "what kind of person am I?" informs a lot of your decisions when it comes to personal style. Since your style is a form of self-expression, you should make sure that it communicates your identity very well. The answer can be something simple like, "I'm a creative person." It can also be very detailed, such as, "I'm someone with a very formal work environment, but I prefer comfort outside of work."

Your assumptions with regard to your personality will then

eliminate a lot of the clothes you already have. Perhaps you love color and prefer loud, bold hues when it comes to fashion. If so, having some "classic" pieces may not suit you at all regardless of common wisdom, like a white tee, black pants or even the signature little black dress.

It can even extend to areas that are more intangible. Let's say you identify as environmentally and socially conscious. Then you might be compelled to only have items that are locally-sourced, fair trade, second-hand or made with recycled or recyclable fabrics.

Practically speaking, you should also consider the climate of the place where you live. While you may like the thought of walking around in a sleek trench coat, you may be in a hot climate where wearing such a piece would be highly impractical if not impossible.

Conversely, if you live in areas with fluctuating climate, then you will need to consider a rotating capsule wardrobe for the spring/summer and fall/winter that will swap items in and out depending on the need (most likely when it comes to footwear and outerwear).

Another factor about your lifestyle of course has to do with your work. What is your work environment like? Are you required to wear formal clothes? If so, you may want to invest in a suit and patent leather shoes. Or perhaps you're a freelancer who works from home. If so, you may not need any formal pieces like blazers, button-down shirts or tailored trousers.

Finally, think back to your favorite things to wear. What kind of clothes are those? What do you like about them? If given free rein, what would you prefer to wear and why? Your goal when it comes to curating your wardrobe should be to capture as closely as possible the way you feel in your favorite clothes. That's what would make having a minimal closet practical, easy and desirable instead of limiting or diminishing.

Knowing Your Aspirations

Now, let's get to your goals. Why are you interested in a minimal wardrobe? What do you hope to achieve? Your aspirations will define your priorities later on when you have to sort out your clothes.

One of the reasons people cite is practicality. Having a limited number of pieces makes fashion decisions easier. In this case, you need a capsule wardrobe that is highly flexible; where everything can be mixed and matched with everything else. It will be streamlined and cohesive but may force you to be unable to follow trends or pick bolder choices.

Another goal is to make better shopping decisions. You're probably familiar with the feeling of having "nothing to wear" despite a jammed pack closet filled with clothes. If you feel out of control financially, having a minimal wardrobe will force you to invest in quality pieces that you can wear more for longer, and not fast-fashions items that quickly fall out of style or get ruined quickly. As an additional challenge, you can opt to not shop for anything until you wear out that item in your capsule wardrobe.

Perhaps you're starting on a new job and you want to look very adult and refined. Therefore, you would need classic pieces like a crisp white button-down, tailored pants, cashmere jumpers and a camel coat. On the other hand. it could also be that you want to be more stylish and experiment more when it comes to fashion. In that case, you can keep some basics and then pad up with other pieces such as modern or sculptural accessories or bolder outerwear. You can introduce new fabrics or cuts into your closet as well.

Altogether, this step will crystallize in your mind what you want out of your wardrobe. Now, it's time to solidify it and start sorting clothes.

3 - Decluttering

It's highly unlikely that anyone can truly be starting from scratch when it comes to fashion. Of course, you've come to accumulate clothes throughout life. Take everything out of your closet, dressers, and suitcases and place them all in one place.

Now, it's time to get them all and sort them into types: shirts, dresses, pants, coats/outerwear, underwear, sportswear, accessories, jewelry, footwear, etc. Finally, you now get to categorizing, the most basic of which is keep, try, sell/donate and recycle/trash.

Keep

When it comes to this pile, be brutally honest. These are the clothes you are guaranteed to keep and will make up the bulk of your capsule wardrobe. Upon first pass, try and keep a number in mind and stick to it. Let's say, strictly keep 50 items only. You can go through these items a second time with stricter guidelines of preference, lifestyle and goals to further pare it down.

A handy guideline is to ask yourself if you've worn this item in the last 3 months. If not, you probably don't like it anymore and are just holding on for no reason. Inertia will be your enemy if you let it. Be strict, be honest and only keep the essentials.

Try

Undoubtedly, you'll come across some items you aren't entirely certain about. For one thing, perhaps it doesn't even fit you anymore. For these items, put them together in a pile and be sure to try them on and then categorize accordingly. Don't get caught up in trying to fit items in. "These pants will fit me if I lose 5 pounds!" If it doesn't fit, get rid of it.

Your capsule wardrobe is for your real self, living your real life. The same is true for items that are too short or too tight. You want to be comfortable in your clothes. That's not going to happen if you're holding on to pieces of clothing that fit your ideal self rather than who you are right now.

If you're unsure because of factors other than fit, then you can keep a "maybe" pile. If within the next three months you find that you had no need to get anything out of this pile, then discard them from your wardrobe permanently as well.

Sell/Donate

For items that don't make your keep or maybe pile, assess if they're still in good quality. If you're looking to make a quick buck, you can hold a garage sale or sell items online. You can also go to consignment stores and have your clothing appraised there. Otherwise, you can also donate.

In order to maximize clothing donation, make sure you're giving away items that are wanted in the first place. For instance, some charities specialize in giving unemployed people formal clothes to wear for job interviews. Some stock up on coats, boots and blankets to give away during the winter. For novelty items like costumes, you can ask around rental places if they can take it or swap it for something else. You can also donate usually non-reusable clothing like prom dresses or gowns.

Recycle/Trash

Finally, anything you don't want to keep and can't sell or donate should be trashed or recycled where possible. Cotton shirts can first be turned into rags for cleaning. Otherwise, sort items by type and find a place where you can drop off materials for recycling. Most of it will be shredded and turn into stuffing or insulation.

Some are turned into industrial rags. Others are just baled and sold by weight. While very little recycled textile is actually turned into new clothing, at least you'll be thinking about the back-end process of clothes you've bought and will buy in the future.

4 - Defining Your Style

With a pared down closet, you can more easily see which items fall into your personal style. For someone who's employed, for example, you can expect formal or smart items dominating the wardrobe with some casual pieces thrown in for going out during the weekends. Someone with a more expensive lifestyle may have exclusively suits, dress shirts and tailored pants in their wardrobe; casual may mean cashmere jumpers, loafers and cigarette trousers instead of cotton T-shirt and leggings.

Find the Connection

Whatever is left in your closet after your extensive decluttering is guaranteed to be your favorite items; items that suit your preference and lifestyle. While you may not know how to label your personal style yet, now you can easily see the similarities which connect them with ease.

The easiest element to spot is color. Color palettes usually are pretty distinctive of styles by themselves. If your closet is dominated by white, khaki, brown and navy, you're likely to have a more classic, timeless style.

Having mostly black items err on the side of chic and sophisticated, but with some bright and bold colors mixed in black pieces may be the foundations of a more modern, avant-garde style. Earth tones usually dominate the relaxed, Bohemian style while a rainbow of colors fit right into whimsical, more playful and creative styles.

Another style element to be on the lookout for is patterns. Most classic or chic styles tend to favor plain colors over patterns of any kind. If you have patterns at all, it may be on the outerwear only, like houndstooth, pin stripes or plaid. Athletic styles recently favor more graphic patterns or camouflage in a variety of colors, as well as large designer names.

Tartans, gingham, argyle and madras are considered quite preppy and feature in a lot of sophisticated looks. Trendy looks may have animal prints such as tiger and zebra stripes, leopard prints or giraffe spots.

When it comes to item types, you may also find that you're a fan of layering in which case you'll have plenty of basic pieces like tees and tank tops as well as layering pieces like vests, jackets and cardigans or even decorative lingerie, bustier or lace-type items, too. For girls, you may find that you prefer dresses and skirts or, alternatively, pants and shorts only. In which case, you won't be needing any of the other types in your capsule wardrobe since you don't feel comfortable wearing those at all.

In terms of material, natural textiles like cotton, silk, and wool dominate most classic styles. More casual and laidback styles include clothing in cotton, jersey, blue denim and linen. Edgy/subculture styles tend to incorporate a lot of leather, dark and distressed denim and metallic hardware. The bohemian style incorporates a lot of handmade textiles like saris, dyed wool, weavings, and knitwear.

5 - Try on a Label

At this point, based on the choices you made when decluttering and the connections you find in the clothes left in your wardrobe, you may already have in mind what kind of style is your dominant or combination personal style.

Depending on where you look, some of these may go by different (albeit related) names or be combined under one category. Nevertheless, being able to properly label your style will help you going forward in terms of streamlining your style further, branching out to try other styles, or simply be a handy guide when shopping.

Classic/Timeless

A style that has stood the test of time. The classic style tends to incorporate basic and smart pieces that can be dressed up or down. Includes a trench coat, Breton stripe shirt, straight-cut jeans, white button-down shirt, tailored blazer, ballet flats, little black dress and black dress pants.

Vintage

Clothing that harkens back to a time long ago. Usually inspired by fashion from the 20s to the 50s or even up to the 70s. Heavy on lace, floral dresses, silk chiffon blouses, sheer items, cardigans and tights or black stockings. Often styled with vintage necklaces, kitten heel boots and small handbags.

Bohemian

Characterized as "hippie" or "gypsy" looks. Popularized in the 60s and 70s. Emphasis on neutral and earth tones in soft and flowy fabrics. Often feature exotic patterns and textiles in layers. Include maxi dresses, oversized blouses, fringed denim, off-shoulder tops, suede boots, sandals, tunics and furry gilets. Often styled with a head accessory like a headband, bandana or flower crown.

Artsy/Creative/Avant-Garde

Fashion as wearable art. Creative styles tend to dabble in bold colors, mixed prints and patterns and unusual silhouettes. Often cannot be defined by trends as they tend to be ahead of the curve and only subsumed by the mainstream after considerable time. Clothing is often accessories by large, chunky and architectural outerwear, shoes and jewelry.

Casual

Comfort above all else. Characterized as relaxed, laid-back and rugged. Basics include cotton shirts, denim pants, khaki shorts, hoodies, skater skirts, and athletic wear like sweat suits and leggings. Often does not include any jewelry but can be accessorized with a beanie, sun glasses and baseball caps. Footwear could be tennis shoes, sneakers, running shoes or flip flops.

Preppy/Geek Chic

Think school uniform vibes. Characterized as clean, refined and collegiate. Includes blouses and dress shirts, A-line skirts, opaque tights, cardigans, Mary Janes, scarves, headbands, pea and cape coats and thick-rimmed eyeglasses. This style also often includes nautical themes like the Breton stripe, anchor prints/accessories, and loafers.

Chic/Sophisticated

A lot like the classic style, only more high status. Exudes power, wealth and refinement. Designer and luxury brands dominate this look. Most pieces are tailored and custom. Often also monochromatic black and white, with only hints of grey, navy, camel and burgundy as touches of color. Includes custom jewelry, high heels, patent shoes and designer handbags.

Edgy/Rocker

Inspired by subcultures like rock, punk or goth. Casual items are often included but with more graphic statements and heavy use of leather and metal elements. Leather jackets are a must. Black is the most dominant color. Often styled with distressed denim, fishnet stockings, studded belts, jackets and boots, platform shoes and leather pants or skirts.

Trendy

Always up-to-date. Following trends and keeping up with celebrity looks and items inspired by the fashion shows. It may be harder to have this style if you're keeping a capsule wardrobe, but it is still possible if you keep to a couple of basics and have on rotation several accessories instead.

Sexy

Tends to flaunt body shape and feature cleavage, legs, and exposed stomachs. Often tight-fitting, short or low-cut. Includes bodycon dresses, miniskirts, cropped tops, cut-out styles, lingerie, lace and sheer fabrics.

Girly/Feminine

Romantic and sweet. Almost exclusively feature dresses in light or pastel colors. This includes floral designs, frills, ruffles and lace which are often styled with a thin, long cardigan, long necklaces, small handbags, platform heels or ballet flats.

6 - Conclusion

Defining your personal style and curating a minimal capsule wardrobe around it will help you communicate and express your identity, aesthetic and lifestyle clearly and easily. Besides that, it is a practical and frugal way to organize your wardrobe in order to maximize your time and your visual impact. Having a curated closet leads to your signature look; that way of dressing that is distinctive and indicative of your individual personality.

After decluttering your closet, you can focus on paring down what items remain. Try them out and see if there's a particular thing that's missing from your wardrobe. Perhaps you have too many tops but not enough pants or skirts in rotation.

It may be that you don't often find yourself wearing dresses at all. Or it could be that you need less shoes and can take away 3 or 4 more pairs. Perhaps you only have jacket and might need a heavier coat as well. The more time you spend with your clothes, the more you can tailor them to your lifestyle and preferences.

And if you should feel as though your capsule wardrobe has grown predictable or stale, you can always refresh it with new items, or reintroduce items you've kept back. You can keep alternates to basic items like a striped shirt in place of a basic, plain one. If you have a monochromatic look, try picking a certain color to brighten it up.

Deep reds, navy and green go well with a black, white and grey-heavy color palette. Picking out certain materials can also spruce up a look, like picking out a leather item to add masculinity to a very feminine style. Casual clothes can also be dressed up with black heels or a long trench coat. Timeless pieces can be made trendier with the introduction of certain accessories or jewelry.

Even if your personal style falls on a broad category, it is always yours and yours alone. You mix it up with your choices and the way that you mix and match. More than the items in your closet and the price you pay for them, the thing that matters most is that you find comfort in what you wear. Your clothes should comfort you, bring out the best in you and make you feel like your best and most beautiful self. A closet filled with only your favorite and most loved items will bring peace and comfort to your daily life.

Book 3 - Dream Closet

A Step-By-Step Process for Creating the Perfect Wardrobe

(Personal Style, Confident Closet, Dream Wardrobe)

1 - Introduction

Do you often hear yourself say, "Urgh, I don't have anything to wear" while you stare at your closet overflowing with clothes in front of you? Or are you too afraid to open your closet as bits and pieces of your clothes peek from the closet seams?

Do you often find it hard to pick out an outfit to wear? Are you usually surprised every time you open your credit card bill? Do you find yourself with several clothes that you rarely use or some you probably never used and have their tags on?

These questions sound familiar, right?

Now, imagine opening your wardrobe and finding only a few essentials with everything neat and well organized. You will probably be amazed to see how much space your closet has and how little time you need to choose an outfit. Having a capsule and organized wardrobe can give you all that.

A common mistake for women is that they tend to just shop and grab. They buy anything that is on trend, on sale or just looked good on their favorite fashionista. Because of these impulse buys or rash choices, your wardrobe and your wallet usually suffer.

To avoid this, it is important to invest in your wardrobe wisely. Evaluate what you have against your lifestyle needs. Look for commonalities and weed out those that do not belong. While you evaluate, make sure to balance beauty, functionality, and value for money.

These are some of the key areas that this book will touch on. It will provide guiding principles to constantly refer to as you take the journey of curating your wardrobe. It also specifies steps that you can take to help you out in the process.

2 - Principles for Creating Your Perfect Wardrobe

If you are planning to curate your wardrobe but do not have the confidence to do so, the first thing you need to have is a plan. You need a clear set of guidelines to steer you to the right direction, simplify your decision making and redirect you to your course should you slip up and find yourself lost in seasonal trends and sale discounts.

To fine-tune your curating process, familiarize yourself with these key values: quality, personality, comfort, form, function, and versatility. These values will serve as a guide to keep your curating process in check.

1st Principle: Go for Quality

Quality over quantity is an age-old lesson that too many choose to ignore. Sacrificing the former for the latter may grant you satisfaction for getting that bargain or on-trend outfit but you'll most likely have to schedule another trip to the mall only after a couple of wears.

Do not ever compromise on quality. Build a wardrobe of high-quality key pieces that will last you more than just a few seasons. It is a better long-term investment to buy a few high-quality pieces than settling with many low-quality bargains. Here are five other reasons why choosing quality clothing is a good idea:

- Future Savings: it is logical to conclude that if you buy better quality clothing, they should last longer. If your clothes last longer then you would not have to replace them as often which means less shopping and indirectly future savings. Although most high-quality products are expensive most items are sturdier and long-lasting. This is perfect for those that like to save up on personal expenses.

- Cherished purchases: buying better quality items take time and effort compared to just buying the first thing you see. The extra effort means that you are purchasing something that you love, and you know will make you feel good every single time you use it.

With choosing quality items, all these purchases can be your favorite and as a result, you'll cherish and take better care of these items too.

- More Space: You will get more space if you have lesser items. Aside from extra closet space, having fewer items also means less time to spend on washing or caring for your possessions, which, in turn, gives you more time to pursue other activities and interests.

2nd Principle: Radiate Your Personality

Your wardrobe should reflect who you are and your personal style. Finding your personal style can be a struggle but once you develop your own, it'll give you a boost of confidence to face the world head-on and give you the ability to genuinely feel beautiful in what you are wearing.

Defining your personal style is not an easy task; you should know what you truly like and understand what looks good on you.

To help you thru this, you can refer to articles like, "10 things every woman should have in her closet" to reference what fashion stylists suggest having as your wardrobe staples. But do not waste your time trying to fit in the style molds out there. Instead of figuring out whether you are preppy, bohemian or classic, it is better to invest your time creating your own unique look. Create a look that's exclusively you, radiates your personality and then build your wardrobe around it.

Having your own personal style has other benefits:

1. Stress-free Shopping: when you go out shopping, you can go directly to the shops that have clothing that follows your style type. You do not have to spend hours going through several shops just to find "the one." Having your personal style makes shopping an experience and make you add a piece to your closet that makes you exclaim, "This is SO me!"

2. Signature look: Wearing your regular go-to look frequently and sometimes playing them up with statement pieces make you stand out and be remembered. It helps you establish your unique style identity that people can easily associate with you. For example, women associate shift dresses and oversized sunglasses to Jackie Onassis and black cropped pants and comfortable slip-on to Audrey Hepburn. Finding an item that you truly love and including it into your daily outfits will help stamp that identity for you.

Being true to yourself is the single most important thing

when developing your personal style. It is not the designer labels but rather feeling good in your own skin that matters. Your style should celebrate your life; let you express who you are, who you want to be, and make you feel like you are the best version of yourself.

3rd Principle: Balancing Form and Function

Your clothes should be both beautiful and functional. Every item you have in your closet should fit your lifestyle and can be worn repeatedly. Each item you choose should reflect your personal preferences and should also account for proper fit and functional purpose.

Aside from making women feel beautiful, clothes should allow women to move, stretch, and possibly feel as if you could dance in your outfits. Nowadays, clothing companies aim to achieve a balance between form and functionality. It is not sufficient that clothes just grab attention but should also serve a utilitarian purpose.

4th Principle: Stylish Comfort

Uncomfortable clothes make you feel conscious, uneasy, and often distract you from your purpose. Worst, when you feel uncomfortable in your clothes, it shows. Your discomfort and anxiety will be made obvious with your face and your actions. You'll probably spend more time fidgeting, tugging or pulling at your clothes rather than focusing on whatever activity you are engaged in.

If you were out on a date, your companion might feel your uneasiness and mirror it. Instead of focusing on getting to know each other or seeing what an attractive person you are, he's distracted by how uncomfortable you are and how hard you are trying to look beautiful. This may drive your date to call an early night and bolt the first chance he gets.

To avoid situations like this, the rule of thumb should be, "if it does not fit right, if it itches, rides up or slides down – out it goes." Comfort is non-negotiable. It is the key. So, no matter how beautiful a garment is if you feel uneasy while wearing it, take it off and find something more comfortable instead.

Be careful though as you do not want to be too comfortable that you start to look like a slob. Yes, there will be days that you do not care who will see you nor would not mind driving around in your sweatpants. It is okay. There's nothing wrong with that. But, do not get sloppy; be sure to also train yourself to be able to put in an outfit that's comfortable, looks nice and fit for the occasion.

5th Principle: Multi-functional versatility

When adding pieces to your wardrobe, consider how versatile it is. Identify how many ways can you style the garment? Ask yourself if it can cross over from day to night or from brunch to dinner.

To be considered versatile, clothes should be able to work on multiple occasions, outfits and seasons. Other reasons to shift to versatile clothing are:

1. Travel Light: with multi-functional clothing, you do not have to check in nor lug around heavy luggage when traveling. You can easily pack for a whole week with only two outfits! For professionals, having versatile outfits in your carry-on bag is more convenient

than having to wait for your checked in luggage at the baggage claim.

2. More Space: Having convertible garments helps you make the most of your available living space. This is especially true for women who live in New York where space is a premium and usually comes with a hefty price.

3. Best value: Quality versatile items often cost more than bargain items, but it comes with uncompromising quality, best functionality and gives you the best value for your money.

3 - Steps to Build Your Dream Wardrobe

Now that you can grasp the principles to curating your wardrobe, here are some steps you can take to start the process:

1. Create a Pinterest Inspiration Board

Browse Pinterest and gather every outfit that you could imagine yourself wearing. Look into your favorite style icons and pin every image that catches your attention. As the board grows, pay attention to any common cuts, themes and color schemes that appear. Do you see a pattern? You probably do.

Bring them together into a coherent group. Your consolidated board will then serve as the main style direction you will be working with.

You can even make this step more fun by gathering a few friends and make style inspiration boards together.

2. Define Your Style

After creating your style board, put into words what your perfect wardrobe would look like. Describe your lifestyle characteristics, colors, your preferred garments and other adjectives that you want to associate with your clothes. For example, minimal, colorful or neutral are some words that define a color palette you may want.

Your color preferences and style are ever changing. It gets more defined as you get older. For now, define what suits your current situation and work your wardrobe around it.

3. Learn Your Body Shape

Knowing your body shape will help you to pick the clothing cut suited for you. It is ideal to go to a tailor to have yourself professionally measured but you can always do it yourself. To determine your body shape, you'd need to have a measuring tape and a buddy to do it with. Your friend will help you in measuring hard to reach body parts.

You need to measure your upper body, your waistline, and your hips and buttocks.

Body Parts to Measure

- Shoulders: You need to wrap your measuring tape in the widest circumference of your shoulder – that is the tip of one shoulder to the other shoulder and then back to the first point.

- Bust: You need to wrap your measuring tape around your back and then place it in the middle of your chest; where your nipples are. Make sure to keep your body straight and that you are not pressing down your bosom while you do this.

- Waist: You need to wrap your measuring tape around the smallest part of your natural waist. Ensure that you are not holding your breath or any form of cheating while you do this.

- Hips: You need to wrap the measuring tape at the fullest part of your hip. Start at the point just below your hip bone. Place the measuring tape through the largest part of your butt up to your other hip and then bring it back to the first point.

Now that you have your measurements, identify your body type to understand the best clothing styles for you:

- Hourglass body type: your shoulders and hips are balanced. You have a very defined waistline that gracefully curves out to your hips.

- Inverted triangle body type: your shoulders are wider than your hips. You have broad shoulders, an ample bust or a wide back.

- Rectangle body type: your hips and bust are balanced. You do not have a defined waistline and your bottom is flat rather than round

- Pear body type: Your hips are larger than your bust. You have a defined waistline. You usually first gain weight in your bottom and legs.

- Apple body type: Your shoulders and hips are about the same size.

4. Define your color palette

You probably already have an idea of the colors that you find attractive, that you like to wear, and what you think looks good on you. But if your friend asks you to name your color palette, she will most likely just see a confused look on your face.

Choosing colors for your outfits is so natural that you do not pay attention to details like that. But defining your color palette will make creating your dream closet easier to reach.

To define your color palette, first, refer to your inspiration board. It should have a collection of images that inspire you. Include a selection of outfits and any random images that catch your attention. Then, edit the collection by removing elements that no longer speak to you. You can also start adding new ones in time.

After reviewing your inspiration board, identify the exact context you want to create the color palette for. Specify if it's only for a single outfit, a seasonal wardrobe or your general personal style.

Then, set your collected images and look for common shades and themes. You can write your own color descriptions, or you can use an online image color picker to get the exact shades. The more specific you are in your color descriptions the better. You can also search for different gradations of the same color to give options for the dominant theme in your collection.

After you have identified your colors, the next step is to organize these colors into a coherent color scheme. There are different ways to build a color hierarchy but the simplest to follow is to differentiate base colors from accent colors.

Base colors are the colors you choose when you are buying essentials. It is suggested to stick to colors that transcend seasons and can be worn for years on end. Common examples are black, white, and khaki. If you wear red every day, you may treat it as a base color.

The basic rule is if you are warm toned, your base color will be solid earth tone, off-white or moss. If you are cool toned, your base colors are gray, navy or taupe.

Highlight colors are colors that are great for mixing with your outfits to update it and keep it in season. As you work with your capsule wardrobe, you can purchase a few colored items each season to refresh and spruce up your collection.

5. Tidy Up Your Current Wardrobe

This will probably be the most difficult step in the whole process. Going through your closet and taking out anything you do not absolutely love.

Here are some questions you can ask yourself while going through your closet:

- Does it fit?

- Is it damaged or stained? Will you get it repaired this month?

- Is it flattering on your body?

- Have you worn this item in the last 12 months?

- Is it a special occasion outfit?

- Is it still in style?

- Does it have sentimental value?

- Is it one of your top 5 sentimental outfits?

- Is it part of your job uniform?

- Can you be convinced to get rid of it?

- These questions have a yes and no option. At the end of it, the choices are either to keep, sell, swap, donate or trash the item.

6. Have a Versatile Base

Using your color palette, select the clothes with your base colors and identify those that can be used as accent colors. By this time, you should already have a basic capsule wardrobe to work with. When you purchase new items, make sure that it is a flattering color, has the perfect fit and can be partnered with jewelry and shoes that you already own.

7. Have Pieces for Layering

Every great wardrobe has a collection of layering pieces – t-shirts, tank tops, cardigans, a couple of jackets, blazers or vests are must-haves. Lightweight sweaters can be worn over tanks. Belts can transform shift dresses into different looks by adding a layered cardigan or a long vest and belting them.

8. To follow the Trend or Not?

It is okay to have trendy items in your wardrobe since trends keep you looking relevant. Just make sure to pick them mindfully. Do not follow trends blindly as you probably did in the past. See if the trend suits your body shape or the new color trend complements your skin tone. Keep impulse purchases in check and make that you only purchase that you truly need.

9. Keep Your Balance and Follow Your Lifestyle

Make sure that your wardrobe does not only have your personal preferences but should also include lifestyle essentials. If you live in the city and mostly walk around to get to your destination, it is best to invest in mostly flats and a couple of heels for special events. If you have the luxury to be driven around or drive, you can stock up on high heeled stilettos.

It is important to also balance your wardrobe staples. If you have a lot of dresses and leggings, do not forget that you might need jeans at some point. Keep a pair for just in case situations. Even if you only wear them rarely, you should have one to keep a balanced wardrobe.

10. Make a statement

Not all clothes must be basic or functional. You can add flair to a simple outfit by accentuating them with a statement piece. Invest in items that are unique, remarkable, makes a statement, and never goes out of style. Make sure that your statement pieces the things that truly complete your personal clothing collection.

4 - Conclusion

By now, you should be able to have a better grasp of what is required to help you curate your wardrobe. Creating your dream closet is a long and strenuous process. The temptation of buying new, exciting, and fashionable clothes will always be just around the corner.

Just remember that the goal is not to have a closet full of clothes, but rather to look good, feel comfortable and ooze confidence. The key to getting these three is having a well-curated wardrobe.

Through curating you learn to prioritize quality over quantity. You develop a good style which is a skill that can be applied regardless of quantity. And you learn to balance the need for beauty, comfort, and value for money.

Book 4 - Confident Closet

Your Guide To A Perfect Wardrobe (Capsule Wardrobe, Wardrobe Building, Comprehensive Guide)

1 – Introduction

More and more people are now slowly moving away from hoarding trendy clothes and are now embracing the practice of creating capsule wardrobes.

A capsule wardrobe is a concept that has stormed the fashion and minimalism world when it was first introduced and it continues to generate interest.

A capsule wardrobe encourages people to declutter without having to go out of style. The way capsule wardrobes work is very simple – you must set a certain limit to the number of items you have in your closet and make sure that you don't go over that limit.

Once you have done this, instead of having a closet filled with a ton of used and unused clothes, you will have a small collection of curated pieces (capsules) that are wearable for your climate and your lifestyle.

Once you have built your own capsule wardrobe, getting dressed in the morning would not be as difficult as it used to be because all your options are laid out to you in an organized way.

There are no strict rules for building a capsule wardrobe.

Some could limit themselves to only 20 closet items, while some must have 50 due to the different activities they have in their regular lives that require them to have different clothing types. But it's not just about the numbers.

The goal, really, is to become more mindful of the things you put in your closet. A capsule wardrobe is more than just having a few pieces in your closet; it is about creating a mindset of prioritizing needs over wants.

If you ever decide to start your own capsule wardrobe, start by asking yourself, "How much of my clothes can I keep without being inconvenienced?" Before buying things, ask yourself, "Do I really need this or do I want to buy it because it is on sale or on trend?"

2 - The Concepts

Before you decide to keep some old pieces or buy anything new, here are a few principles that you must know and understand when creating a capsule wardrobe.

Fit

The first and most important thing you must keep in mind is how the clothes you want to keep or buy fit on you. No matter how good and fashionable an item looks like, it will always look bad if it does not fit you well. Once you discover the type of fit you want, you are one step closer to building your capsule wardrobe.

There are a few things you must consider before you decide to keep an article of clothing or before buying a new one. You must check if the shoulder seams hit the tip of your shoulders, and make sure that the clothes you choose fit your body's form. Do not keep or purchase clothes that are too tight or too baggy.

To help you get your perfect size, take your measurements and check if the clothes you want are of the same size. This can be very difficult to do since clothes are usually not made to perfectly fit all body types. The important thing is to find the size that fits you well, and not force a certain garment on you just because it is in style or on sale.

There will be instances when wearing loose clothing actually works. But it is important to really think it through so that you do not waste money, time, and space. Discovering what type of clothing really suits your style can be a long process – some people prefer really fit clothing while some like more airy and loose ones. This is something you must experiment on once you finished gathering your basic pieces.

Simplicity

One of the main things beginners find difficult to do is simplifying their outfits. People usually tend to over-complicate the items in their wardrobe by keeping a ton of colorful clothes that are difficult to match. No matter how good the fit of your clothes are, if they are too colorful or have too many patterns, you will have to let them go eventually.

The simplest items are more lasting – they can be mixed and matched to give you the best look. Start by picking subtle pieces, such as those with subdued colors. These color options are more versatile, so you can easily match and re-wear them without being too conscious about repeating your clothes.

Earth colors such as navy, tan, and green are easier to work with than bright yellows, blues, and reds. This does not imply that you must entirely get rid of all your bright colors, but it is important that you know how to work with them.

Another classic example is using a range of dark color tones, such as grey, white, and black. These are the go-to basic colors for people who want to minimize the bulk in their closet by switching to capsule wardrobes. Dark color tones are so easy to mix and match without having to look boring.

As a general rule to going basic, you must learn to combine tops and bottoms that make a nice contrast. For example, you can wear dark pants with a light top to create a simple contrast. This principle could also be applied when you want to layer some clothes. Simply pick clothes with slightly different color tones – such as matching a light shirt with a dark jacket.

The contrasting principle can also be applied to different textures. A smooth cotton top can be paired with a wool cover up to create some contrast even if the colors are quite similar.

Once you have mastered the basics, you can move on to exploring other color palettes. You can start incorporating monochrome or grayscale looks into your closet. You can even add a few textures and patterns once you have developed the skill of matching things. Eventually, you will discover your personal style while still maintaining a wardrobe filled with only the essential pieces.

3 - Clearing Your Current Wardrobe

Before you can start building your own capsule wardrobe, you must first clear out your current closet to make space for new pieces and keep old ones that are still useful.

Step 1: See

Start by taking out all the clothes, shoes, and other accessories that you have in your closet and put them on the floor (or your bed). Take everything out, and don't leave anything behind. They must be placed on your floor or bed so that you will be forced to finish the decluttering immediately.

An important part of building a capsule wardrobe is seeing everything that you currently own. Being able to look at all the things that you have acquired, how much you spent on clothing, and which one of those you never even wore could be a great eye-opener. It will make you realize that a lot of the things you buy and keep are things that you do not even use.

Step 2: Sort

Once you finished staring and contemplating about everything that you stuffed in your closet, it is time to get the work done. Begin by sorting your clothes into piles. Don't think about it too much; just go with your gut feeling. If you pull a top and you immediately think that you won't wear it ever again, then it's time to let it go. You can sort your pieces by dividing them into these separate piles:

- Love - These are items that you wear frequently and love too much. They fit you well and are still of excellent quality so you can wear them multiple times every month.

- Maybe - These are items you want to keep but are still unsure of the reason why. You can set them aside for a while, but know that you must get rid of them if you realize that you will not use them no matter how much you like them.

- Donate - These items are those that don't have the right fit but are still very useable.

- Trash - Items that are in very poor condition must be

thrown away. If they have sentimental value, you can repurpose them.

Once you have finished sorting everything, pack up the "donate" and "trash" pile and set them aside. Try on your "maybe" pile and think of the following questions:

- If I saw this in the store today, would I still buy it?

- Will I still wear this in the next 3-6 months?

- If your answer to these questions is no, then add these items to your "donate" pile.

Step 3: Choose

Create a list of items that you want to keep by category. Start by choosing items that you use regularly. This list can change over time, especially when significant changes in your work or life occur.

You can make a list of clothes that you want to have in your wardrobe such as jeans, shirts, blazers, button-down tops, and dresses and skirts for girls. You can also keep a few basic and valuable jewelry and other accessories. For your shoes, you can keep some flats, slippers, sports shoes, and heels (if you're a woman).

4 - Building a Capsule Wardrobe

Now that you have decluttered your current wardrobe, it is time to build a new, more organized and simple one. Here are a few ideas that can guide you when looking for basic clothing. One of the most important things you must remember is to take your time. Contemplate about how you can work with the items you see and how long you can use them.

Once you are convinced with an item's versatility, that's when you take it. Being cautious of the things that you buy can help save you from being frustrated about failing to accomplish your goal of minimizing your wardrobe items. This guide is broken down into sections and is made for living in a place with a number of seasons. If you live someplace that is mostly warm, you can disregard the cool weather suggestions.

Warm

During warm seasons, it is important to own tops with light colors. Getting crewneck tees in solid plain colors such as grey, white, and other natural colors must also be on your list. These tops are perfect for layering or for general wear.

If you find items with minimal texture or a few simple designs, that would also be a bonus. Just make sure that these items still have that simplicity that you are looking for so that you can re-wear them often.

For polo shirts, pick well-fitting and simple ones that have no bold patterns on them. Polo shirts with solid plain colors could go well with several bottoms and can be paired with most jackets.

For shirts, casual button-down shirts are items that you must keep an eye on. They are simple yet stylish, and they can be paired with anything from jeans, shorts, and skirts (for girls). Shirts with neutral colors are more preferable because of their versatility.

If you want to add a little visual interest to your wardrobe, then add in some linen shirts and patterned tops like striped or polka-dotted shirts in simple and subtle colors.

Cool

When the temperature gets colder, this is the chance for you to experiment with different textures. You can start by picking out flannel shirts – they are warm, soft, and casual. Most flannels come in plaid patterns, but do get one in a solid color if you find any that fits your size and taste. Flannels are the perfect basic casual top for cool weathers.

If you are looking for a warmer top, then start hunting for an over shirt. They are thicker and heavier since they are made of wool or heavy flannel. Overshirts are not really a necessity, but they can be a great alternative to jackets and sweatshirts and are preferred by some people.

In case you don't want to get an over shirt, sweatshirts or hoodies are great options. Find those with simple colors such as grey or black. These shades are extremely versatile and can go well with anything. You can keep it in your car and wear it multiple times in case the weather gets a bit cooler.

You can also explore on a few more colors like red or blue, as long as they are still simple and subtle. Just remember the principles of contrast before purchasing a more daring color.

If you want to get something thicker, look for a thick crew neck jumper made of wool. This also has a number of color options, but it is best to stick with natural and basic tones (olives, greys, browns). Sticking to these color palettes will keep you looking good and extra warm without appearing too overpowering.

Bottoms

For your bottoms, a number of staple items are things that you probably already have.

First on the list are jeans. Choose items that are clean and basic, such as plain dark indigo jeans. When picking your jeans, it is important to focus on the fit. Try on a number of pairs until you find one that fits you perfectly – allowing you to move freely and comfortably. Your preference for how your jeans fit is really up to you. Some people prefer slim, skinny jeans, while some like bell bottoms and high-waist ones.

Once you have found the best blue jeans, it's time to move on to looking for the best pair of black jeans. Getting black ones are equally important for more basic options in your wardrobe. Black jeans are also versatile and are easier to match with lighter tops and shoes for better contrast.

Chinos are the next thing that you must look for. These are flat fronted trousers usually made from cotton twill. It is best if you get one in navy and tan so that you can have a pair of bottoms for light tops and for dark ones. Chinos can come in very handy during times when you have to dress up.

Once you have accomplished these basics, you can explore more interesting pieces like light stonewashed jeans. These can be paired perfectly with darker tops, especially during the summer. However, you must keep in mind that the color and fit of this type of jeans must be carefully considered to avoid looking distressed.

When the weather starts to get extremely warm, it's time to look for some shorts. Get ones similar to how you picked your chinos – flat-fronted, simple, and versatile. Be sure to fit them and choose one that you know you can use again for the next summer.

If you're ready to add a little more adventurous piece in your wardrobe, you can start looking for slim-fit cargo pants or wool trousers. Just be sure that you will be using them a couple of times.

Shoes

Your shoes are a huge maker or breaker of your outfit, so you must be able to get ones that would complete your look.

It is important to understand that when picking the right shoes, the idea of simplicity must be your guiding principle. Shoes that are overly decorated can appear very messy and can only be used once or twice in your lifetime.

For sneakers, it is essential to find ones that are simple with a clean design. A basic white sneaker is a perfect match for most outfits, and it provides a great contrast to your jeans. Grey sneakers are a good alternative, especially if you are the clumsy type that always gets your shoes dirty. It is also easy to match and is very versatile.

Another good shoe investment is a pair of boots. Getting leather ones are the best choice. The simpler the better, so avoid getting those that have dangling charms and other designs on them. Plain leather boots are perfect for the winter and can be matched with almost anything – so you can wear them every day.

Another type of shoe that you can add to your collection is leather shoes. Picking the right ones can be very subjective, but it is highly recommended that you get simple brown ones. They can go well with almost everything, even shorts.

Now that you have read the basic guidelines for building

your own capsule wardrobe, it is time to put them into action. Always keep in mind the basic principles of contrast, subtleness, and simplicity, in order to look your best in the simplest way.

5 - Conclusion

A capsule wardrobe is a good investment. If you have been overwhelmed with a ton of stuff that has filled your life (and your wardrobe) and have forgotten the things that really matter, then clearing your wardrobe can be a great start to reconnecting with yourself.

Living with less and dressing up through a few important pieces will help you discover that there are a lot of things that you can get rid of so that you can make more room for the things that matter.

Deciding on what you should wear every day can be a very stressful task, especially when you are already late for work and you still have to dive into a pool of clothing to find your favorite plain white button-down top. By building a capsule wardrobe, you won't have to hunt for clothes and try on several outfits to find the perfect one to wear.

Having a capsule wardrobe means having your clothes laid out to you in an organized way so that you are wearing the things that you love every day. You might not realize it yet, but by dressing with only a few pieces to choose from, you will have more time and space to do other things.

No matter how big or small your closet is, your life will be made simpler if you have solid pieces in your wardrobe. Having only a few basic items that you can wear all year at any weather will make you feel assured that you won't need to keep buying things when the new season comes.

These clothes may not be the latest trends, but these are classic pieces -- basic, lasting pieces that can easily be combined to keep you looking stylish. If you are going to spend on clothes, invest on the classics.

In case you are having doubts about creating a capsule wardrobe, write down the reasons you wanted to start doing it. Understand how it will help you not only clean out your closet, but also help make your life better.

Thank You

As we reach the end of this book, I want to say thanks for reading this book.

I want to get this information out to as many people as possible. If you found this book helpful, I would greatly appreciate you leaving me a review. This helps others find the book as well.

Disclaimer

This document is geared towards providing exact and reliable information in regards to the topic and issue covered. The publication is sold on the idea that the publisher is not required to render an accounting, officially permitted, or otherwise, qualified services. If advice is necessary, legal, financial, medical or professional, a practiced individual in the profession should be ordered.

This information is not presented by a financial or medical practitioner and is for entertainment, educational and informational purposes only. The content is not intended as a substitute for professional medical advice, diagnosis, or treatment. Always seek the advice of your physician or other qualified health care provider with any questions you may have regarding a medical condition. Never disregard professional medical advice or delay in seeking it because of something you have read.

The information provided herein is stated to be truthful and consistent, in that any liability, in terms of inattention or otherwise, by any usage or abuse of any policies, processes, or directions contained within is the solitary and utter responsibility of the recipient reader. Under no circumstances will any legal responsibility or blame be held against the publisher for any reparation, damages, or monetary loss due to the information herein, either directly or indirectly.

Last Updated: 3.Sep.2018